TOC Thinking

TOC Thinking
Removing Constraints
for Business Growth

Yishai Ashlag

Additional copies can be obtained from your
local bookstore or the publisher:

The North River Press
Publishing Corporation
P.O. Box 567
Great Barrington, MA 01230
(800) 486.2665 or (413) 528.0034
www.northriverpress.com

For more information on the concepts
presented in this book, please visit
goldrattconsulting.com

ISBN: 978-0-88427-206-9

Printed in the United States of America

About the Author

Yishai Ashlag holds a PhD in economics from Bar-Illan University in Israel. Upon graduation, he spent a year as a post doctorate visitor at the Wharton School at the University of Pennsylvania. For the last 20 years, he has worked as an adviser, consulting government agencies, policy makers, investors, and businesses in various sectors such as automotive, consumer goods, agribusiness, healthcare, finance and retail. Ashlag, worked closely with the late Dr. Eli Goldratt, the developer of the theory of constraints, and is also his son in law. Currently he is senior partner at Goldratt Consulting; where he acts as the head of knowledge development and implementations.

Foreword

"How much time do I have?"

Dr. Eli Goldratt was my father-in-law and my best teacher. And he had just learned that he had stage four lung cancer.

The doctor tried to convince him to fight, but he cared about only one thing.

"There is one more book that I want to write. I need to know if I have enough time."

He didn't.

The book he wanted to write was about management philosophy.

Management is a practical subject. Philosophy is perceived as the opposite.

Why a book about management philosophy?

Philosophy is about a point of view, perception, the spectacles through which we see the world. It's the attitude we adopt toward problems, conflicts, opportunities, risk and uncertainty.

Having the wrong attitude can get us very busy generating modest success. We tend to put a lot of emphasis on ideas, tools, tips that we can use, success stories that inspire us. Yet we tend to devote little attention to examining and defining our approach in generating the desired results. How are we aiming to succeed? What is the philosophy behind the way we work to achieve success?

In business, as in sports, the focus is on winning. But great teams and great companies are about more than delivering immediate results. They have developed their unique core philosophy that makes them great over time. When the emphasis is only on winning by delivering the numbers, companies are likely to compromise on the development of their philosophy and its application.

This book is not an attempt to write Dr. Goldratt's book, but an effort to reveal his philosophy through 15 subjects. Each subject is an individual branch of the same tree. Each can be read alone, but together they portray a more complete perspective. The first six chapters highlight the major management errors we tend to commit and their implications. Chapters 7 to 15 elaborate on the building blocks of Goldratt's approach to sustainable growth and success.

Goldratt's books have sold millions of copies, yet he was not completely satisfied. He felt that people were fascinated with the new tools and solutions he provided, but they didn't realize the principles behind them, principles that should help them create new tools and solutions. I hope this book will help to make his vision a little more viable.

Table of Contents

1

The Goal

"The ultimate goal is to create harmonious and sustainable growth"

When we think about business growth we tend to focus our attention on a new big idea, a new vision as a path to success. Then, full of enthusiasm, we charge forward to pursue this vision. But most often this is not the way to start. The starting point of this quest is not moving forward with the things we should do, but rather stop doing the things we should not do.

Our organization is already preoccupied with many initiatives that are not necessarily promoting us in our quest for successful growth. Some of these initiatives may be even holding us back. So starting by launching more grand initiatives is probably not the best idea. The first step in the process of creating harmonious growth is to examine our rituals, behaviors and activities in order to identify the ones which exhaust our time and energy without getting us closer to our goal. We need to look for the policies and processes that make us, as managers, very frustrated.

It is relatively easy to list the processes and rituals that frustrate us. We know them well as most of them have probably been part of our organization's reality for quite a while. The question is, how are we going to stop them, how do we dismantle long standing repetitive behavior? The answer does not lie in the specifics of our situation, or the details of our organization, but in the understanding that it is a generic problem. A problem that exists in almost every organization. There is something common and generic in our way of thinking as managers that leads us astray. There are common management errors that consume a lot of time and energy. Errors that frustrate us and block our path to growth. Understanding these errors is critical to freeing up the management capacity that is required to focus on our goal.

Identifying what we should not do and stop doing it is the first challenge. Once we free the management capacity the next challenge is how to focus this capacity toward our goal. Typically we start with a vision that may look very clear, but as we translate it into intermediate objectives and operational needs we find ourselves with many conflicting requirements, where people and functions pull in different directions. "The enemy of the good is the best". This means that seeking to achieve the best results may prevent us from achieving a good enough progress. But how do we know when we should compromise, when "good" is enough or when we should insist on exceptional results? How do we get the different functions of the organization to agree where we should compromise and where not, and work as one toward the goal?

The key to creating focus is to understand what the system constraints are. On the strategic level what constrains the creation of the exceptional value for our customers and on the operational level what constrains the system from accelerating the flow. Addressing these two questions will help us not only focus and synchronize the different functions but also solve many of the perceived conflicts.

The general connotation of the term "constraint" is negative. The Theory of Constraints suggests an alternative perspective. The system's constraint is actually the leverage point. Once the system goals are well defined, understanding what the systems' constraints are is the key to building the game plan; the strategy and tactic plan that will get us moving toward our goal.

2
Dealing with Uncertainty

"Don't force certainty on uncertain situations."

Reality is full of uncertainty. Yet managers are expected to deliver certain and predictable results. In order to increase the chances of success we need to incorporate uncertainty into our planning and monitoring tools. Unfortunately, the conventional tools for budgeting, forecasting and detailed planning do exactly the opposite. Each of these tools uses projections to force the illusion of certainty and accuracy on uncertain situations, which masks the uncertainty instead of highlighting it.

Accuracy gives us a false sense of security. It implies that the variations are small when in reality they are much larger. For example, when it is expected that a given project will cost $10,250, it is implied that the expected variation is in the hundreds of dollars. In reality, the variation can be in the thousands. The project might cost anything between eight thousand dollars to twelve thousand and even more. Providing a number that is more accurate than the noise doesn't really add any beneficial data. It just gives a false sense of certainty and misleads us.

Since uncertainty cannot be eliminated, fluctuations in results are unavoidable. When we hold people accountable to detailed forecasts we ignore this basic truth. Thus, when we find that the forecast is met to the second decimal point, it is most likely that someone has played with the numbers.

By acknowledging the unavoidable fluctuations in results, we can achieve meaningful improvement by making sure that our improvement efforts have much bigger impact than the impact of the noise/uncertainty. We have to understand what the noise range is and make sure that the expected impact is outside this range.

Projections of future demand are used to plan most of the supply of goods. The longer it takes to produce a product the more has to be assumed about the demand. For example, it takes an average of three months to produce a watch from sourcing of components to delivery to the stores. Therefore watch manufacturers use this forecast in order to project the demand in three months, and plan their supply accordingly. The performance of the supply chain operation is measured by the alignment to forecast. It is typical for a watch manufacturer to reach an alignment to forecast of 85%, which is reasonable taking into account the different disturbances in sourcing and operation. The real problems are exposed not when we look at the alignment to forecast but when we look at the alignment to actual demand.

A mass watch manufacturer has an average of 1500 models. There are men's watches, women's watches, youth watches and more. Each of these categories has various styles, from sporty look to elegant; different shapes; different sizes; different colors and finishes. Accurately forecasting the demand for all these combinations three months into the future is impossible; definitely not at the store level, but also not at the regional warehouse level. The typical outcome is a shortage level of 50% at regional warehouses coupled with 30% non-moving inventory. At the store level the situation is even worse. Therefore even when the watch supplier insists on getting firm commitments to buy from the stores, the problem has not been solved. It is just pushed to the stores. But once the stores get stuck with the wrong mix the whole supply chain is suffering. We just can't effectively mitigate the impact of uncertainty with forecasts and firm commitments.

The right approach to mitigate the impact of uncertainty is to reduce the supply time. This is achieved by holding inventories in aggregation points along the supply chain. Aggregation of demand calls for a central warehouse where the variations of local/regional demand cancel each other. Excess demand for a specific model in one region is compensated for by less than average demand for the same model in a different region.

Aggregation of supply calls for holding inventory before diversion points in manufacturing. For example, in watch plants, inventory of watch cases should be held before case plating. A given case can have different finishes. It can be gold-plated, metal or black finish. By holding the components before assembly, and specific components like cases before plating, where they will be committed to a particular style, we can shorten the time it takes for manufacturing to respond to actual demand. Applying these principles results in reduction in supply time from three months to fifteen days, which is the waiting time for assembly and shipping time to the distribution point. The level of shortages falls accordingly from 50% to 15%. Non-moving inventory is almost eliminated.

The mistake of using detailed projections to force the impression of certainty on uncertainty is not limited to supply chain. Similar mistakes are made in business planning, project management and finance.

In project environments the instinctive reaction to uncertainty is detailed planning. The notion is that the more detailed the plan, the less we leave to chance. The result is a large network of activities, which sometimes number in the thousands. But no matter how detailed the plan, it cannot make the uncertain certain. The detailed plan just gives us a false sense of accuracy and predictability.

When the plan is very detailed, we actually review and monitor tasks and activities that are much smaller in duration than the impact of the noise/ uncertainty on the schedule (for example, if the tasks we monitor are four to five days long while the project is eighteen months long and may run late by six months). This is the opposite of focus. Instead of putting all the attention on the source of uncertainty and its actual impact on the project's progress, we monitor thousands of tasks whose potential impact on the schedule is negligible. The potential impact of these small activities is within the noise.

Another common policy that forces the impression of certainty on uncertain situations and gives a false sense of security is holding every task in the project to a committed due date. When people are pushed to give a certain date, they give a conservative estimate with some internal buffer or padding hidden inside it, which is an additional time for safety between the average expected duration and the committed date. These hidden buffers are not part of the plan, and, therefore, are not managed and eventually misused.

In the effort to force certainty, managers take actions that hide the uncertainty rather than expose it! The right mode of operation is to have a formal time buffer as part of the project plan, and manage the consumption of this buffer against the progress of the project. An increase in the consumption rate of the buffer provides managers with the focus on the spots where the impact of uncertainty is the most significant.

When uncertainty is high (like the development of a new drug or a new market), time and resources for iterations should be part of the plan. When starting new business initiatives, we tend to underestimate the number of iterations that are needed.

The combination of uncertainty and dependencies causes chance to be against us. One late task is enough to make all the dependent tasks late. Therefore it is important in the planning stage to take action to reduce dependencies at critical points. Some of the dependencies are created artificially. For example, the dependency between engineering and procurement. It is common for procurement to wait until all the technical drawings are done before they start sourcing. Although this helps avoid excess purchases, it may inflate the overall project time considerably. In many cases this will result in financial losses that are much greater than the procurement savings.

The stock market represents all the ills of forcing the illusion of certainty on uncertainty. The way we trade allows prices to fluctuate within the noise. No one can estimate the value of a given company with the accuracy of one to three percent. But we have no problem letting the price fluctuate even by a tenth of a percent. The daily change in most stock prices is within the noise. In the current mode of operation the stocks are used as noise generators to enable the traders to make a profit by the end of the day. The problem is that when we react to noise, the noise level tends to increase. This should make economists think again about their assumption that the more we trade the more efficient the market is. It might be exactly the opposite.

Analysts are also caught in the game of forcing certainty on uncertain reality. They publish estimates for quarterly results and expect the companies to meet or beat them. These estimates are also known as "Wall Street consensus expectations." This is definitely a myopic approach, which eventually increases variability. Usually there is a big time gap between when the company is at risk of losing its edge and when actual sales are affected. When sales are affected it is already too late: the stability of the company is already compromised.

Expecting a company to meet a quarterly estimate is no different than expecting every task in a project to be finished in a pre-defined time. In both cases we use projections to force certainty on uncertainty, giving a false sense of control. Actually, this mode of operation masks the uncertainty and eventually increases it.

3
Dealing with Conflicts

"The fear of 'tug of war' causes managers to look for compromise instead of solutions."

Facing a conflict, our natural instinct is to look for compromise. This tendency is helpful with day to day minor conflicts. But the more significant the conflict the more the instinct to look for a compromise is counterproductive. We need to look for a solution to remove the conflict and reach a higher level of achievement.

In general, we deal with three different types of conflicts: 1) internal conflicts in situations where we face conflicting requirements to achieve our objective; 2) conflicts with other functions in the organization; and 3) external conflicts with vendors or clients.

The way we deal with conflicting requirements is known as "optimization." But optimization is not a solution. It is merely the best-known compromise between the conflicting requirements. Only for mathematicians is optimization a solution to a problem. It is only a solution on paper. In reality we have to look for an assumption we can challenge in order to break the conflict and find a solution.

In the supply chain there is a common conflict about the level of inventories that we should hold. Holding too little inventory may compromise product availability and service level. Holding more inventory may compromise inventory turns and return on investment. Optimization is the compromise between these two needs, finding the right trade-off between the sales loss due to poor availability and the impact of the additional inventory on the return on investment. A solution calls for change in the supply mode, so with smaller inventories we can support a higher level of availability. This typically calls for higher frequency of replenishment coupled with holding inventory at aggregation points.

Product design is also a place where we tend to do a lot of optimization, but the real breakthrough comes from finding a solution. The evolution of the smartphone is a good example. For a while the major conflict was about how to divide the space between the keyboard and the screen. Almost every manufacturer introduced several models with different compromises between these two needs in an effort to accommodate to different customers' preferences. The touch screen solved this conflict and very quickly became the predominant configuration for every smartphone.

Conflicts with other functions in the organization usually trigger a lot of emotions. Our tendency to blame the other side blocks us from finding a solution. If we keep insisting that the source of the conflict is the other side, there is very little we can do about the situation at large. Thus it is to our benefit to assume that people are good; that it is not the other side's "bad character" or "stupidity" that has created the conflict. But rather, the conflict arises due to something in the particular situation in which we are caught.

Having the right attitude when approaching a conflict is necessary, but not sufficient. To find a solution, we need to differentiate between the actions that are in conflict and the needs they aim to satisfy. Our solution is a new mode of operation that satisfies both parties' needs without compromise.

Defining the conflict clearly is the first step toward finding a solution. Goldratt suggested using the following template to assist us in describing the conflict:

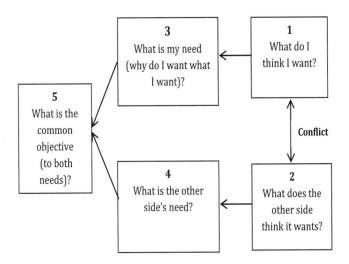

Answering these questions allows us to define the conflict so that we can start looking for a solution. A solution is defined as finding a mode of operation that will satisfy both needs. To find this new mode of operation we need to challenge our assumptions about the relationship between the actions we want to take and the needs we aim to satisfy.

Is what we have proposed the only way to achieve our needs? What in our desired action specifically jeopardizes the other side's needs? Can we modify our action/process so that both needs will be satisfied? What other factors will significantly affect the actual result? Once we add more dimensions to the problem (i.e. how to satisfy two needs, and what will affect the level of satisfaction), a new mode of operation is likely to arise.

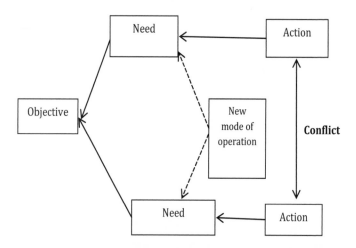

When the conflict is external (with vendors or clients), we often try to negotiate a compromise in our favor. The problem is that even if we succeed, a win-lose situation is not a stable solution. It deteriorates over time to lose-lose. This argument requires an example.

The U.S. jewelry retail market consists of thousands of family-owned stores. Traditionally, jewelry retail is a slow-turn business. The average inventory turn is less than one. The stores tend to have a long tail. Thirty to forty percent of their inventory is over a year old. The problem is that the stores mainly sell fresh inventory. As a result, the stores ask the vendors to exchange merchandise. The conflict is about the terms. The stores wish to exchange one for one. Otherwise, over time they will inflate their inventory, which will result in an even larger tail. The vendors wish to have a one for two or three exchange ratio. This way the new purchase by the store "subsidizes" the cost of exchange and the potential loss of melting the gold jewelry. The common practice is an exchange ratio of at least two to one.

It seems, at first, that the vendors get it their way. But the implications of this policy have a negative impact on the vendors, too. The stores tend to wait as long as possible before they ask for an exchange. As a result, the exchanged items are out of fashion and have a small chance of getting resold. The stores that are caught in this situation also avoid reordering. They wait on reordering until they have an exchange deal. As a result, the stores run out of fresh and fast-selling items. Not only do the stores lose sales but the vendors end up selling less than they might have as well.

One vendor from Sunrise, Florida, decided to break this conflict and find a win-win solution. This vendor provided stores with a program whereby the stores can exchange one for one during the year if the stores do the reordering at the time of sale. This way the stores get what they want: no dead stock cluttering the store and no need to inflate inventory. The stores can exchange any item any day as many times as they wish with no penalty of having to buy more. The vendor gets what he wants: the additional sales from frequent reordering cover the cost of exchange and more. In addition, the ability to exchange one for one at any point of time leads to better interaction with the stores and enables the vendor to exchange slow-moving items before they become obsolete. When the exchanged item is part of an ongoing collection it has a high chance of finding a store that will order and sell it.

The longer a given conflict exists (which we might call a chronic conflict), the harder it is to find a solution, since it becomes increasingly more difficult to differentiate between needs and actions/ policies. Over time these two elements become one in our minds. Political conflicts, as an example, tend to deteriorate into chronic conflicts. Unfortunately, many times, it takes a disaster to make the public reevaluate what its real needs are. When politicians talk about values, they highlight the importance of the need for which they advocate. Such politicians are not in the business of finding solutions. They prosper with conflict.

4
Dealing with Complexity

"People fear complexity and admire sophistication (perceived complexity), both of which have negative consequences."

Complexity slows us down by limiting our ability to use our intuition. The higher the complexity, the higher the chance it will delay us from achieving the results to which we are committed. As managers we strive for simplicity. The problem is that too often our attempts to simplify reality end up creating more complexity.

The fear of complexity causes managers to break an organization into smaller units. We assume that smaller units are simpler to manage, since it is easier to obtain focus and rely on our intuition in decision making. But this attempt to simplify reality usually comes with a big price tag. Breaking the organization into smaller units requires more synchronization efforts, and thus increases complexity. It also promotes local optimum behavior, which makes the organization less focused.

An example of the tendency to break the organization into small units is described nicely in Ford's CEO, Alan Mulally's book, *American Icon*. Soon after he took over, Mulally realized that there was not just one Ford, but many. There was Ford of U.S.A., Ford of Europe, Ford of Asia and a host of other divisions and subsidiaries. And there was little coordination, or even cooperation, between its many parts. Mulally's first priority was to weld these separate regional divisions together into a single, global enterprise. In an early meeting with reporters, Mulally was asked if he was interested in a merger. "Yes!" he exclaimed. "We're going to merge with ourselves."

The fear of complexity also causes managers to deal with problems in isolation. When facing a problem, managers tend to look for a confined solution within the area where the problem lies. For example, in operations it is very common to deal with productivity, quality and safety issues separately as if they were unrelated. The perception is that trying to find a root cause may open a Pandora's box of difficulty. Different functions may need to be involved. Finger-pointing is likely to happen. Dealing with each problem in isolation makes it easier to demand accountability. We ask the responsible function to provide a solution to the problem in its area. But this course of action is unlikely to make a significant overall improvement. When we deal with each problem in isolation, we deal with symptoms—not the real cause. As long as the real cause is untouched, the symptoms/problems will not go away, and, even worse, new ones may be created.

The tendency to deal with symptoms rather than the core problem can be demonstrated by looking at the retail fashion industry. One of the key areas of concern is markdown policy. End-of-season sales are critical for clearing the stores, but they also have a severe negative impact on margins. Retailers tend to look for the discount model—an algorithm that will guide them based on sales rate, inventory level and other factors that determine the right time to discount and by how much. This kind of optimization can't provide a real solution. It tries to address directly one of the negative ramifications of overstocking rather than dealing with the root cause and preventing it. Retailers have a natural bias to overstock, simply because one can't sell what one doesn't have. But since only a limited part of the range becomes a best-seller with meaningful sales, filling the stores with a wide range and too many multiples in one or two shipments in a season is bound to create a lot of excess, aged stock that will eventually compromise sales. The solution to all these undesirable effects depends on dealing with the root cause and changing the supply processes. The right processes call for frequent introduction of new merchandise and frequent replenishment, coupled with special emphasis on protecting the availability of best-sellers only.

To create simplicity managers need to take a holistic approach. We have to manage the organization as a whole toward one goal. It is the deeper understanding of how the organization is going to achieve its goal that creates simplicity. This understanding enables us to build and put the right processes in place to support the organization's strategy. It also enables us to identify and create a consensus of the root causes for the undesirable effects in the environment and to focus the improvement effort around these areas.

5
Sophistication

"In the same way that accuracy is used to mask uncertainty, sophistication is used to mask a fundamental misunderstanding of reality. People have developed a fascination with sophistication, as it is assumed to be a proxy for intelligence."

We find sophistication in all three management errors:

- We force certainty on uncertainty by excessive accuracy

- We force compromise on conflict by excessive optimization

- We force simplicity on complexity by excessive specialization

Excessive accuracy, optimization and specialization are the major elements of any sophisticated solution. Sophisticated solutions tend to use statistical tools to provide accurate answers. Sophisticated solutions also tend to use advanced math to solve optimization problems. Moreover, these solutions tend to address problems that are defined too narrowly due to over-specialization. For example: Trying to define the right end-of-season discount policy instead of finding ways to prevent overstocking. Or, trying to answer how to maximize resource utilization while the important question is how to increase the overall flow. The prevailing paradigm in social science in general, and in economics in particular, suffers from all three manifestations of sophistication. Economics suffers severely from excessive specialization by creating many narrowly defined fields. It also suffers from excessive accuracy and optimization by the use of overly sophisticated mathematical and statistical tools.

We tend to believe that in order to achieve a breakthrough in business we need a sophisticated solution. In reality, only seldom are breakthroughs based on a sophisticated approach. Instead, breakthroughs depend upon the ability to successfully challenge a fundamental assumption in the industry. The problem is that challenging assumptions is a risky business. Uncertainty is frighteningly present. Sophisticated solutions carry the false promise of certainty. We tend to assume that whoever came up with the sophisticated solution knows what they are doing and thus will deliver. Experience, however, doesn't support this assumption. The knowledge and skills (in math and statistics) that are used in sophisticated solutions are almost always a commodity. The value that such solutions provide is almost always overestimated.

Examples of sophisticated solutions that have failed to deliver can be found in areas such as forecasting, planning and finance. For a long time, forecasting future demand provided promise to manufacturers who struggled with oscillations in demand. Sophisticated statistical tools were used and models were built in an effort to predict the near future demand based on historical data and patterns.

However, despite these efforts, oscillations, which resulted in shortages and surpluses, still occurred. The breakthrough came when Jay Forrester showed that most oscillations are created by the suppliers' behavior, not the market. It was the switch from pushing inventories down the supply chain to a pull-based replenishment mode of operation that eliminated inventory cycles in most industries. As for planning, the rise of computer power in the 1980s created an expectation that sophisticated planning and scheduling algorithms would improve manufacturing productivity. A slew of software companies entered this field, but most of them met with relatively mild success. The breakthrough in this area came when Goldratt showed that bottlenecks are the focal points for regulating and increasing the flow. Releasing work orders in line with bottleneck capacity prevented overproduction of non–bottlenecks, resulting in smaller queues and shorter lead times. Opening the bottlenecks' capacity and reducing set-up time helped to increase productivity considerably. Implementing these changes didn't require a computer or a smart algorithm. It required a change in the mindset of how we view production.

The history of finance is full of examples of sophisticated products that ended in disaster. Derivatives are the most notorious. Warren Buffett once called them "weapons of mass destruction of capital." Derivatives were created initially to enable the holder of a risky asset to hedge against risk. For example, a wheat farmer and a miller could sign a futures contract to exchange a specified amount of cash for a specified amount of wheat in the future. Both parties have reduced their future risk: for the wheat farmer, the uncertainty of the price, and for the miller, the availability of wheat.

The story loses its pastoral innocence when we begin to trade the contract itself. The first challenge is to determine the derivative price. What should the price of a contract whose value is derived from an underlying risky asset be? Myron Scholes and Robert C. Merton had the answer. They developed what is known as the Black and Scholes Model. The model describes the mathematical relationship between the current price of the underlying asset and the derivative price. Their sophisticated solution was a great success and led to a boom in derivative trading. Within two decades of the introduction of their model the total volume of derivative trading was bigger than the volume of stock and bonds trading. By that time, derivatives were not being used for their original purpose of hedging. Instead, they were being used for taking larger and larger bets. Scholes and Merton's contribution to the development of the derivative market was acknowledged by a Nobel Prize in Economics in 1997. Ironically, the year after, the hedge fund the two gave their name to lost $4.6 billion and triggered the largest bailout at that time.

What went wrong? The sophisticated Black and Scholes Model is based on the assumption that uncertainty has a normal distribution. As Nicholas Taleb showed in his book, financial assets tend to have a fat tail. This means that assuming normal distribution greatly underestimates the risk. Here we have another form of imposing false certainty upon uncertainty. We impose a known bell curve distribution on unknown distribution. As long as we don't experience a tail event, everything looks fine. The model appears to work. When a tail event happens, we call it an outlier, or a "perfect storm event." But as Taleb showed, such events occurred too often to call them one-time accidents. The magnitude of derivative trading and the counter-party risk hold the whole financial system hostage in case of tail events—and therefore force a government bailout.

Since derivatives' pricing models force certainty on uncertainty, derivatives are priced in a way that present risk as smaller than it actually is. This attribute was used in the events that led to the meltdown of the financial system in 2008. Credit derivatives were used to present riskier loans as safer than they actually were. This helped to fuel the subprime market, and created a tangled network of credit default bets that amplified the risk in the markets. The story of the financial crisis has been told by many; the point here is that our admiration of sophistication made us blind to the risk. Nothing much changed after the crisis. Faulty cars trigger a recall, dangerous products like cigarettes are sold with some restrictions; but derivatives are still traded in the same fashion.

Sophistication in finance is the way of doing business. Money is a commodity. Profits are made from trading risk. Sophistication is used to present the level of risk as predictable and therefore as smaller than it actually is. This eventually increases the risk in the markets.

If you are approached with a sophisticated solution, you can be certain of one thing: It is most likely a solution to someone else's problem, not yours.

6
Management Attention

"Management attention is the ultimate constraint of the organization."

The ultimate constraint of any business is not money or a machine or technology. It is not even the market. It is the management's ability to generate the desired results. Managers are always looking for more time to deal with the issues knocking on their door. Even when we look at the most successful companies, where resources are not an issue, we will find that the company doesn't have the bandwidth, or management attention, to grow at a faster pace.

Management attention is consumed by the effort to achieve the desired results while dealing with three main challenges: Uncertainty, Conflicts, and Complexity. The bigger the presence of these challenges, the harder it is to achieve the organization's objectives.

There is a common conceptual mistake we make in the way we deal with these three challenges. Too often we try to force the desired results in spite of the challenges, rather than creating a reality in which these challenges are solved, or at least better mitigated. This approach causes us to:

- Ignore the inherent uncertainty by relying on detailed projections instead of highlighting the uncertainty and trying to minimize its impact by creating a robust plan/ structure.

- Accept an unsatisfactory compromise instead of finding a solution to the conflicts.

- Circumvent the complexity by focusing on performance of subsystems instead of understanding how to manage the system as a whole.

The problem with this approach is twofold. One, we leave the exposure to uncertainty, the existing conflicts and the level of complexity untouched, and as a result we limit the potential for improvement. Two, as time goes by, the level of noise created by these challenges tends to increase, and we find ourselves spending more and more time fighting the fires that result from these challenges. This firefighting ends up consuming and wasting large amounts of our management capacity and jeopardizes our ability to focus.

Examples of the above tendencies can be found in every aspect of the business. We use projections and commitments in an effort to contain uncertainty, but this approach often causes a situation in which we take distorted actions to meet the commitment. This phenomenon is known as "end of the month syndrome."

We produce in large batches to meet the production quota, even though the production is not aligned with actual demand. We push a lot of inventories to big accounts to meet the sales target, even though it compromises the availability of the ideal product mix. Facing a conflict, we look for a compromise. But the compromise is usually not stable over time. We experience oscillations that are created by the ongoing changing compromises, such as increased overtime or reduced overtime; increased product range or shrinked product range; do more sales promotions or protect the brand by minimizing sales promotions.

Breaking the organization into subsystems usually ends in conflict between the different functions. Sales' typical complaint to Production is "why can't you produce what we can sell?" Production would ask in return: "why can't you sell what we have produced?" Similar conflict can be found also between engineering and production. "Design a product we can manufacture" versus "manufacture the product to our design specs." Every time we manage by functions and not by processes, we create more conflicts like these.

There is another aspect that is common to these three management errors: the overemphasis on outputs like sales and production targets, and less of an emphasis on the inputs, or the capabilities that are required to deliver the results. In the name of meeting our targets we tend to try to force results in spite of the challenges ahead. For example, when we rely too much on sales promotions to achieve our sales target, rather than improving the appeal of our offering. Or when we introduce too many new products to the point of saturation. We try to get sales from smaller and smaller niches rather than broadening the appeal of our main offering. In production, over-emphasis on achieving production records is usually a sign of trying to get over, rather than solving, the challenges that compromise the flow. To deliver immediate results, managers tend to put emphasis on production records. But to consistently improve production, the emphasis should be on the inputs: improving lead-time set up, opening bottlenecks, reducing dependencies with full kit.

The conceptual mistake of trying to plow through challenges rather than solving them is not limited to business. We often see this behavior, for example, in the way that some governments and central banks operate. When a central bank reduces interest rates from low to very low in an effort to achieve the desired growth target, the bank is making exactly the same mistake. The level of interest rates was not the obstacle for growth. But by lowering it again and again the central bank hopes to create enough momentum in the economy to bypass the economy's real problems. It is trying to artificially force its growth expectations on the economy while ignoring the real constraints that hinder economic growth.

After two decades of such an approach we begin to witness the rise of the anti-growth movement. But growth is not the problem. The problem is the way we often try to achieve it.

The right approach to dealing with the three business challenges of uncertainty, complexity, and conflict is to address them as part of an overall business strategy. If management attention is the ultimate constraint, it makes sense to focus on that. We can't split our attention between the way we aim to achieve the results and the efforts to deal with these challenges. We should look for a business strategy that aims to achieve the desired results while creating a reality in which the challenges are removed—or at least reduced to a manageable level.

The key is to have a business strategy that aims to deliver exceptional value to customers. When we focus all our attention on how to deliver exceptional value we deal with all the multiple challenges simultaneously. This way we deal with the external challenge of separating ourselves from the competition, and at the same time we use the goal of exceptional value to focus the organization on building the required assets and processes to deliver that value. This helps to synchronize the different functions and breaks the critical conflicts that can jeopardize the delivery of the value.

7
Value

"Value is created by removing a significant limitation for the customer, in a way that was not possible before, and to the extent that no significant competitor can deliver."

The common definition of value is the ratio between the features and benefits of the goods or service to its price. In accordance, any additional feature or benefit increases the value. Since not all features have the same merit in the eyes of the customer, different levels of superlatives to describe the value, such as "good," "great," and "exceptional" are used.

Great businesses are built around the idea of delivering exceptional value. The question is, how do we know what exceptional value is? The answer is that this kind of value is created by removing a significant limitation in a way that was not possible before, and to the extent that no significant competitor can compete with.

Companies thrive in the periods they are able to do exactly this. Prominent examples are companies such as Walmart, IKEA, Google, and Apple. For Walmart, the concept of an "everyday low price" enabled many families to stretch their family budget. IKEA was the first to offer contemporary furniture at very affordable price points. Google considerably improved our access to information and advertisers' access to their targeted audiences. Apple used tight integration between software and hardware and its ability to cooperate with media providers to simplify the way we consume digital entertainment.

When assessing value we have to be careful not to put too much emphasis on market surveys. Most often, customers take limitation as part of reality. They don't foresee a reality without limitation, and therefore are not in the best position to evaluate new possibilities.

Traditional strategic thinking focuses on analyzing the competitive landscape (known as "Porter analysis"). This forces us to focus on the competitive position too soon. When we do this, we "put the carriage before the horse." We must first and exclusively strive to understand the value we plan to deliver, rather than think about how to protect our business. When we start with competitive analysis, the main focus is on how to limit the competition, using vertical integration and high switching cost, and we are less likely to come up with a vision of exceptional value. Moreover, it is the quest to deliver value that generates the assets that then create the competitive edge.

There are four major layers of protection that are created in the pursuit to deliver value: paradigm shift, leadership position, unique processes, and benefits of scale.

The first roadblock to competition is a paradigm shift that is required in the way a company operates in order to deliver value. To remove a serious limitation for its customers, the company needs to challenge some of its assumptions about the way it does business. The more fundamental the assumption, the higher the chance its questioning will lead to a paradigm shift. In general, people do not like to go through paradigm shifts, as such shifts take them out of their comfort zone. Many of the rules they have relied on are not valid after this shift, and new rules need to be established. It is the company's ability to go through these paradigm shifts that gives it the lead in the new market.

Similar ways of thinking about business strategy are described in W. Chan Kim's book *Blue Ocean Strategy*. To demonstrate this point, let us review the companies in the previous example. Walmart had to challenge the industry pricing and merchandising policies. In the effort to reduce its product price points, IKEA challenged the assumption that furniture should be assembled before being sold. It required a clear vision of value to so vigorously insist on this policy. Google introduced the search page format during the time that "the gate" to the internet was a Yahoo-style portal.

Apple didn't invent the MP3 format or player, but it was the first to offer an MP3 player with a web store to buy music. Apple insisted on selling songs for 99 cents when the industry consensus was that the right model was renting the music for a monthly subscription fee. The "experts" viewed the subscription model as the answer to the music industry problem. Apple believed that the 99 cent model was the answer to the consumers' need to own their music and therefore was committed to the model even though it complicated its billing system with micro transactions. Later, when Apple introduced the iPhone, it challenged the grip on access to content that the cellular providers held. In less than five years it forced the industry to change its practice and open access to the web.

The paradigm shift associated with delivering exceptional value is just the first challenge for competitors to follow. Delivering exceptional value usually redefines the market and positions the company that introduced this value as the market leader. The combination of being a market leader and the time gap it takes the competition to go through the new paradigm shift puts the company in an excellent position to capitalize on its value offer and expand its market and reach. Simultaneously, the company has to develop special processes that will support such rapid expansion. These processes together with the benefits of scale help the company foster its competitive position.

In the current example, Walmart developed its

own processes for efficient replenishment, mass employee training, and opening new stores.

IKEA's design process starts with the target price and accommodates materials, logistics, labor and transportation costs to support it. No other furniture retailer has such a unique and holistic process. With their successes, both Walmart and IKEA enjoyed the economies of scale.

Google built a local, national and international distribution network for AdWords, the company's main advertising product. This operation is no less exceptional than its searching algorithm.

Apple relied on four fields to support its growth: The ability to put together media deals to add more and more digital content to its iTunes store; the ability to develop and introduce new and improved products to maintain its product leadership; the ability to source and manage an efficient and responsive supply chain; the development of its unique retail concept and the concept's deployment. One or two of these elements would be enough to secure a leading position in the market. Having all four makes it very hard for the competition to play catch-up.

If we wish to evaluate the potential value of new technologies, we can also benefit from Goldratt's definition of value. Typically, we try to evaluate the potential value of the technology by estimating the potential value of the functions and features that the new technology provides. This kind of analysis tends to be murky. In isolation, some features may only have a small benefit, and it is hard to assess the value of the features combined.

When the criteria involves the extent of the removal of significant limitations, the answer becomes much clearer. It also helps us to focus on what other changes in the business' policies are needed in order to actually remove the limitation. In many cases where a new technology can reduce a limitation, there are fundamental changes in policies and norms that are required in order to materialize the value. We tend to underestimate the challenges in changing these norms and policies. For example, we see the changes in norms and policies the music industry had to go through in order to capitalize on digital music. Similar examples can be found in healthcare, defense, or any other industry. The following process guides us step by step from the power of the new technology/what the technology actually does, to the value it aims to provide and the challenges to delivering this value:

- What is the power of the technology / application?

- What current limitation/barrier does it eliminate or vastly reduce for the potential customers?

- What policies, norms and behavior patterns does the current market use to deal with the limitation?

- What new behaviors will the customers need to adopt in order to reap the benefits of the new technology/application?

- In view of the above, what changes and/ or additions to the new technology should be introduced?

- What are the major roadblocks to change?

8

Growth Strategy—Viable Vision

"Build, Capitalize and Sustain are three elements that each growth strategy should contain."

Organic growth strategy starts with a vision. This vision is comprised of a unique value that the company wishes to provide and build a successful business around. Creating exceptional new value commands numerous, and sometimes fundamental, changes in the various parts of the business. On the other hand, to smoothly deliver the value, execution seeks stability. The challenge facing every company that aims rapid growth is how it can maintain growth and stability at the same time. The way to achieve growth and stability is to approach the growth strategy as an act of three major elements: Build, Capitalize, and Sustain.

The first phase is all about preparation: Building the required unique capabilities and assets that are necessary to deliver the exceptional value in the right scale. In this process we build and acquire different assets. These assets may be unique technology and know-how, exceptional operational capabilities or even the number of users (in case of Internet companies like eBay and Facebook). Sometime less tangible, but not less important assets are the unique processes that were developed and implemented in order to deliver the value. The understanding of these processes, and their importance to the company's growth, is what enables management to maintain stability and harmony as the company grows.

The Rydell organization story demonstrates this point nicely. Leonard and Wes Rydell had the vision to change the way customers and employees are treated in the retail automotive industry. The two issues are closely linked. For many years the common practice in the automotive retail business was that employees were paid based on what they produced. Sales people made their income based on how many cars they sold and for what margin. Service people compensation was closely linked to the amount of maintenance work they completed and billed. These practices eventually gave the automotive retail business its negative reputation. It induced a reality where sales people used negotiation technics to land the client on a vehicle that made the most amount of money for them, and a maintenance visit typically ended up with an inflated bill.

Rydell wanted to create a business that is built on trust and a long-term relationship with the communities its dealerships are operated in. Rydell's first move was to make all its dealership negotiation free. The sticker price was the price for every customer. Sales reps compensation was changed so that the margin on the vehicle was not part of their consideration anymore. Service technicians got paid by the hour and not by how much work they billed. This all sounds very noble, but it presented an enormous managerial challenge. Dealerships (like investment banks and accounting firms) are used to relying on incentives to manage, and suddenly all these incentives had to go. The close link between income and expense was loosened. It became much easier to put the dealership into loss. And in addition there was also a need to manage the change. As negotiation was thrown out of the window, many sales guys found themselves out of their element and many of them left.

To address these challenges Rydell had to develop and install a new operating system in its dealerships. A new, negotiation free, sales process had been developed. To maintain productivity with the absence of the common incentives, processes to manage sales force, maintenance workshop and body shop had been developed and implemented. It was a difficult journey and Rydell knew it takes the perspective of an owner, who can see the long term benefit of this approach, to go through these challenges. Rydell presented its store managers with the opportunity to become store owners. From modest start with two stores, the Rydell organization grew in two and a half decades to almost 100 stores. In its annual conference you can see many people who joined this journey and vision from the very bottom and over the years became successful store owners. And for the industry, a lot of the concepts that were pioneered by the Rydell organization were adopted by many other dealers. Today a significant number of dealers in the United States are negotiation free, or what is known as "best price" dealers.

The second phase, capitalization, is all about creating a successful business around unique capabilities and the value they provide. This means different challenges for different companies. For consumer goods companies, the main emphasis is on marketing. How do we communicate the new value and new possibilities this value brings? What are the right references for value and price? How do we get third parties to cooperate? There is more than one way to address these questions. Different companies may successfully adopt different approaches. For example, Lifeline and Life Alert both pioneered the US medical alert service with great success by providing elderly people with panic alarm buttons that enable them to call for help in distress situations. Yet they took completely different approaches in the way they built their businesses around basically the same service. Lifeline relied on affiliations with healthcare providers to get most of its customers, while Life Alert acquired its customers mainly through a direct response channel, and it is known for its iconic tagline: I've fallen and I can't get up! Despite the very different marketing and sales approaches, both Lifeline and Life Alert reached similar results, sharing the same dominant position in their industry. How to capitalize depends many times more on the organizational culture and approach rather than on finding the right analytical answer.

For retailers, the main task in the capitalization stage is how to expand the branch network. Capital is almost always an issue; but mass training of employees is also often a major challenge, just like in the Rydell story. For companies that sell projects or are part of a supply chain, the main challenge is sales. The sales force has to learn how to depart from selling products to selling solutions and unique offers. Taking the jewelry example from previous chapters, the company had to teach its sales people how to shift from selling fashion jewelry to selling the program and servicing it. For Internet companies, the main challenge in capitalization is usually finding the right business model. How can the company make money from its customers without upsetting them? Facebook struggled for a long time with the question of how to capitalize on their mobile users. Addressing these challenges leads to new know-how, which means that more critical processes have to be defined.

To sustain the growth we have to prevent future

roadblocks. When the company experiences enhanced growth, the first cracks appear in operation. The system has a hard time coping with the rapid increase in demand. To be prudent, the company has to plan its operation to deal with the negative consequences of success. However, sustainability is not just about securing smooth operation. To prevent marketing from becoming the constraint, the company has to work continuously on creating new value for both existing and new customers. When companies fail to do that they eventually lose their relevancy and their customers. The challenge with creating new value is that in the process and in the name of providing more value the company can become unfocused and end up in a number of markets/segments where it provides mediocre value and generates modest results.

It is easier to avoid this pitfall if we keep Goldratt's definition of value in mind. Value is created by removing a significant limitation to an extent no other can. Providing more value without losing focus can be achieved when the company concentrates on removing the same limitation to a higher degree over time. The anchor is not the technology or the know-how the company possesses, but the limitation it aims to remove to a higher degree over time. Finding the next jump in performance is a challenge. Flourishing over time is a difficult task. Staying committed to a given vision of providing extraordinary value to consumers' needs can help us avoid jumping to the wrong place.

9
Process

"Process definition requires more than a series of action steps; it needs clear documentation of the relevant whys and hows."

Processes are the backbone of every company's operation. They are the basis of scalability. Having the right processes in the key parts of operation is what gives the company the ability to maintain stability while growing. It is human nature to look for shortcuts. Therefore, processes tend to gradually evaporate. To avoid process evaporation and costly re-implementations, organizations spend a lot of energy on follow-up to make sure that processes will be followed "by the book." Sales process training is a good example. Successful auto dealers put a lot of emphasis on it to the extent that it becomes part of their daily management routine. They learned that good training increases customer satisfaction and sales people's productivity. It also reduces their turnaround.

As we strive for ongoing improvement, some existing processes have to be challenged. Sometimes, changes in the business reality also mandate changes in some of the organization's processes. Thus, we face the challenge of having to play by the book and rewrite some parts of the book simultaneously.

Armies rely heavily on the idea of following the process by the book. This provides numerous examples of the danger of following processes blindly out of inertia. The American Civil War presents probably one of the gravest cases. It was the deadliest war in American history with the death of an estimated 750,000 soldiers. This death toll accounted for 10 percent of all Northern males 20–45 years old, and 30 percent of all Southern white males ages 18–40. The American civil war was one of the early modern wars in the sense that it was comprehensive and included civilians and not just a small professional army. This war also saw the introduction of new rifles and bullets, with faster reload, better accuracy, and the ability to cause greater physical damage.

Yet the generals following their formal training and their Mexican war experience used the tactic of advancing in shoulder to shoulder formations of two ranks at a rate of no faster than 454 feet in a minute. This tactic was very effective with slow reload inaccurate rifles. It enabled the creation of a line of fire without taking too much heat from the opponent. But as rifle technology improved this tactic became obsolete. Failing to recognize the potential impact of these changes in time caused many soldiers to march to their death.

Process follow up is critical for success. But following it blindly is dangerous. The way to examine which processes should be kept without any deviation and which should be challenged is to document the process in a way that combines the processes with the logic behind those processes. It is the ability to check the assumptions behind the process that enables good process audit.

There are two different kinds of logic that need to be documented along with each process. The first one is the logic behind every step in the process, or, in other words, the reason that every step is needed. The second rationalization addresses how a given process is in line with the overall business strategy and the value the company aims to provide. This validation is very important since often processes that make sense on their own contradict other processes in the organization. In these cases, the processes are defined too narrowly in the attempt to optimize sub-system performance. This creates operational and business conflicts that hinder system synchronization and performance.

In order to properly document and audit the organization's processes, Goldratt introduced a logical tool known as the "Strategy and Tactic Tree," a logic tree that ties the organization's strategy and its key processes together. The starting point—the highest level of the tree—is the organization's ultimate goal. Every level down in the tree represents an intermediate objective toward the organization's goal, as well as the tactic used to achieve this intermediate objective. It usually takes six levels to fully describe the connection between the ultimate goal and the complete set of processes necessary to achieve this goal.

Unlike conventional thinking, which maintains that the strategy is the higher objective, and positions tactics as the list of activities to achieve it, the Strategy and Tactic Tree defines strategy and tactic as pairs in every level. In every level we ask what our strategy is—what is our objective and what is the tactic we must use to achieve this strategy? Every page in the tree has the following format:

Necessary assumption: explain the need for this step and its strategy

Strategy: what is the objective or state of being this step is trying to achieve

Parallel assumptions: explain why the tactic achieves the strategy. What are the key assumptions that make the tactic effective?

Tactics: the mode of operation required to achieve the strategy.

Sufficiency assumptions: why there is a need to

go another level down and define another level of intermediate objectives. What is the main challenge in creating the mode of operation as written in the tactic?

Whenever the company adopts a strategy that is based on delivering new value, constructing the Strategy and Tactic Tree is especially important. Delivering new value puts the company in unchartered waters, as the ground rules are not yet well defined. Typically the company relies on the ability of key people to use their intuition to deliver. To empower others to perform better and to make the business more scalable we must translate this intuition into logic and construct the tree. This is critical for both education and empowerment. But it also benefits the person who had the great intuition to start with. Intuition is the beacon that precedes the logic. As our understanding grows, so does our intuition. Thus, when we are forced to teach others and to turn our intuition into logic, we simultaneously improve our own intuition.

CarMax is a good example of a company that put an emphasis on highlighting the logic behind its process. CarMax was developed by Circuit City in 1991 with the vision of creating an "honest used car business." The excessive bargaining and ne-gotiation in the used car business makes for a distasteful customer experience, giving the whole industry a notorious reputation. CarMax aimed to change all that. Yet changing was far from easy. If you read the company annual reports from its early days you can see the challenges and obsta-cles management was facing. Used cars by nature are not all the same. There is no "factory" for used cars. How does the company buy the right vehi-cles? To what level should the vehicles be recondi-tioned? Used vehicles also depreciate on average about 2% a month. How does the company man-age its inventory to limit depreciation risk? What is the right negotiation-free sales process? How can trades be dealt with without overpaying for them and without upsetting the customers? The answer to all these questions could not be copied from any existing textbook. CarMax managers had to write their own. With some level of trial and error CarMax developed its unique processes to address these issues, and many more. These pro-cesses provided CarMax the base for growth and the required stability. Today CarMax is the largest used car retailer in the US, operating more than 100 branches, and is a Fortune 500 company. Car-

Max has been named "America's Most Admired Company in Automotive Retailing." It also has been on Fortune's "100 Best Companies to Work For" list numerous times.

10
Focus

"Focus is not just what to do, but mainly what not to do."

The most important part of focus is to have a set of clear criteria to determine the following: which opportunities the company should pass up on; what the company should let other companies do since this opportunity is not in line with the value the company delivers, the unique processes in which the company excels, and the growth strategy derived from all of these elements.

Focus is not about just saying "yes" to the right things, but more importantly saying "no" to many good opportunities we encounter. Goldratt used to describe these opportunities as "golden traps." He especially disliked mergers and acquisitions opportunities. He saw them as major source of distraction from building real value. Goldratt's reasoning was based on the first century Roman philosopher Seneca, who defined luck as an opportunity that met preparation. You can expect to have luck on your side only when the opportunity matches what you have prepared for. Any opportunity that distracts from the unique value, processes and assets you build is not really a special opportunity for you and is likely to defocus your business.

In execution, all three management errors—forcing certainty on uncertainty, forcing compromise on conflict and forcing simplicity on complexity—lead to loss of focus. The more we rely on detailed projections the more likely we are to lose focus on the real source of uncertainty. We spend our time monitoring large numbers of small tasks instead of focusing on the critical elements of the project and monitoring the impact of uncertainty on them by their buffer consumption. Negotiating a compromise also results in loss of focus. Typically the compromise is not steady. In this case we spend our attention on ongoing negotiation and oscillation between different compromises. Since the compromise is not satisfactory we also spend a lot of management attention on dealing with the gaps between the desired state and the actual results. When we simplify reality and break it into fields of specializations, we increase the chances of dealing with symptoms (undesirable effects) and not the root cause (core conflict). This is the opposite of focus. The same is true when we break the organization into sub-units. We increase the chance that these units will run local goals that are not in line with value the company aims to provide, which is the place on which we want to focus.

In marketing and sales, what prevents companies from focusing is the tendency to put too much emphasis on management by numbers rather than by processes. When management is too occupied with trying to make the numbers, it is easy to drift into additional distribution channels and expand product/service offerings to areas where the company acquires no added value. In operation, what prevents companies from focusing is the tendency to look for improvements everywhere, assuming that any local improvement translates into global/bottom line improvement. To have focus, we need to understand and define what the focal/critical points of the system are. What are the system constraints?

11
Constraint

"In management, constraint should have a positive meaning. It is the key indicator for where and how to focus the organization's improvement efforts."

There is a long-standing debate on where one, or a company, should focus their improvement efforts. Should they sharpen their edge by working on their strengths and make them ever stronger? Or should they strive to improve their versatility by working on their weaknesses? It is easy to argue both ways, depending on the situation the individual or the company is facing. The right and consistent answer is that we should focus our improvement efforts on improving our constraint.

The ultimate constraint of any organization is management attention. But for most companies, there is also something more tangible that limits

its growth rate. The constraint can be found anywhere from marketing, to sales, operation, supply chain, product development, and the market in which it operates. The location of the current constraint shows us where to focus the organization's improvement efforts. The constraint doesn't just indicate to us where to improve locally. It also guides us in improving the synchronization of the different parts of the organization.

The following process, known as the "Process of Ongoing Improvement," aims to help the organization focus more efficiently in its improvement effort:

Identify the system constraint

Exploit the constraint

Subordinate everything else to the above decisions

Elevate the constraint

Return to step one, while avoiding inertia

To identify the constraint, we have to understand what limits the system from achieving its goal. When the constraint is policy, we don't look to exploit it but to change it. In all other cases, we aim to exploit the constraint before we try to elevate it.

To demonstrate this point, let's look at a business that has been under pressure for a long time—the apparel sales catalog business. The apparel sales catalog business saw its best days in the first half of the previous century. Since that time it has been fighting to keep its relevancy. As in many categories, product life got much shorter, and customers changed their buying pattern, buying more often, looking for different and new products each time. A catalog that is published ahead of the season cannot satisfy this need and quickly becomes outdated. The Internet also presents a challenge to the catalog business. It can be continuously updated and opens the door to more competition. The result is enormous pressure on sales. In an effort to stop sales sliding, a common practice is to add more and more pages to the catalog. The direction is one way. Each catalog is thicker than its predecessor, but sales are at best flat. This reality also creates operational challenges. A big part of the inventory is stuck in products that have a very slow rate of sales (tail). The level of shortages is high. On average 30% of the orders are not fulfilled. The apparel business traditionally suffers from big batches and long lead time.

The process of making a catalog also presents business challenges. It takes on average five months to prepare and print it. Thus merchandise presentation is locked much before we get close to the season when the successful trends are more noticeable. It seems that no matter where we look at the catalog business we see many challenges. How do we focus the improvement efforts? One example is a Japanese catalog company that has 10 million people buying from its catalog. So marketing, or the market wasn't the constraint. The margins were also there, but sales were going only in one direction—down. Sales level is definitely the constraint. To exploit the constraint the catalog company focused first on reducing shortages and unfulfilled orders. Most of these unfulfilled orders were for the best selling items, which accounted for 5% to 20% of the range, depending on the category. The company developed several technics to use its website to identify the best sellers as early as possible. Procurement and supply chain worked with key vendors to reduce resupply time. Subordination to the constraint in this case calls for aligning the product range with the actual sales. Since in most categories the range was inflated, it had to be cut. Tactics for liquidation were developed, and money tied up in wrong inventory was released.

To elevate the Sales constraint, the company embarked on an effort to cut the catalog development time from five months to a month. This will enable the company to introduce multiple collections in a given season with feedback from one collection to the other. The vision of the CEO of this company is to turn the catalog into something like a fashion magazine where the customers can buy what they see.

Like fractals that describe the same pattern in different scale, the "Process of Ongoing Improvement" can be applied not just to the organization as a whole but also to a subsystem that aims to improve its throughput.

Exploiting the constraint calls for different actions in different environments. In production, we have to identify the bottlenecks; the resources that don't have enough capacity to deal with actual demand. To exploit the constraint we have to open the bottlenecks' capacity by reducing their idle time. This is achieved by reducing setup time, creating overlaps between shifts and breaks, creating the right priority in maintenance and other supporting functions. In a single project environment the constraint is the critical chain—the longest chain of dependent tasks and resources. To exploit the constraint we have to minimize the waiting time for these tasks. This is achieved by having a project full kit, having the right priority system for resource allocation, creating the right alignment with subcontractors who are part of the critical chain, and having real-time monitoring systems ("buffer management") to minimize response time to disturbances.

When there is a constraint in sales we have to understand the conversion ratio of the different steps in the sales process. Typically we expect to find a step where the downgrade in performance is severe. It can potentially be in a number of stages: creating the trust, building the value, having the right references or dealing with objections. To exploit the constraint we either have to improve the sales process training or modify the sales process so its relevant conversion improves.

Having a constraint in marketing means that creating the required awareness is the challenge.

Exploiting the constraint means focusing on the right message and focusing on the right initial market segment and sales channel. The segment that is more receptive to our message and offer, and the channel that is more likely to accept our offer.

When the market is the constraint, the attractiveness of our offer is the limiting factor. Putting aside a case in which a company dominates its market, this typically means that the value the company provides is questioned. This is a very risky situation. Yet in most cases we can't skip the "exploit" step and try to come up with a completely new offering and value. In the immediate term we have to exploit the constraint by finding unserved niches and support them. This should buy us enough time to come up with a new "blue ocean" strategy and elevate the constraint.

Subordination means aligning the non-constraint elements with the constraint. In production it means limiting the release of work orders to the floor according to the constraint capacity. It tells us when not to produce. In single projects it mandates putting the right buffers in place to prevent the feeding paths from delaying the critical chain.

Subordination in sales calls for controlling the amount of open leads per salesperson. It may also call for modification in the sales process in cases where the sell is done by a team.

Subordination inside a function like production or sales is helpful in synchronizing that function. The broader context for subordination is the synchronization of the complete system. For example, if sales is the constraint, how should production subordinate to that? What changes in production policies are needed to enable sales to sell more? In general we have to understand what determines/constrains the overall flow of the system and align all the parts to support that flow. For example, in retail the flow is determined by the customer traffic. Yet the stores are stocked mainly based on their physical space, which has nothing to do with current traffic level.

When we significantly improve the area of constraint, the constraint is likely to move to a different place in the system. Then we must start the process again and understand that some of the policies and norms we put in place will have to change again. To keep the company stable while growing, the constraint should be kept consistently at one place outside marketing or the market. This place acts as the clock that determines the company's growth pace. Many times there is a gap between where the actual constraint is and where it should be. The constraint should be kept as a key process in the capitalization stage. For example, in retail the constraint should not be in marketing (the chain appeal or value offer), store format, merchandise management, or supply chain. It should be in the pace in which the retailer can successfully open new stores.

12
Flow

"The primary objective of operation is flow."

When we look at the day-to-day management of operations we see multiple objectives that require attention. One objective is the ability to deliver the required output. Another objective is to improve the level of service by improving due date performance and reducing lead time. A third objective is controlling and reducing cost. We also can't overlook quality and safety.

When we look at these objectives in isolation we tend to see conflicts between them. For example, to increase output we often need to save setups, while in order to reduce lead time we need to cut the batch size and increase the number of setups. Similar conflicts occur between cost and lead time, as well as between quality and volume. These conflicts lose their perceived importance once we change our point of view and look at flow as the primary objective of operation. When we focus on the actions that fundamentally enhance the flow we are likely to achieve all the above objectives.

This argument can be demonstrated by looking at the reality of hospital emergency rooms. In the US the average wait in an emergency room is around two hours. The flow is very slow. The average time spent in the emergency room is about four to five hours. It seems also that more doctors and nurses are needed but there is no budget for it. Other areas of concerns are issues like the quality of diagnosis and care and their overall cost. The traditional approach would put the emphasis on cost considerations. How can we save on medical staff and testing cost? But this approach usually creates more conflicts than solutions. A real breakthrough can be achieved when we look at the emergency room flow as the primary objective and start asking ourselves what slows down or jeopardizes the flow?

What creates unnecessarily queues and waiting

time? For example, how many of the non-minor patients got treated correctly the first time. The more iterations we have the slower the flow and the lower the quality of treatment. Looking at local cost in isolation we may advocate that the lion's share of initial diagnosis will be done by junior staff. Understanding the overall impact of mistakes on quality of care, flow and overall cost may change our mind. Having a senior doctor in the initial diagnosis can increase the flow and reduce the overall cost.

Another area that impacts emergency room flow is the waiting time for lab results. Putting an emphasis on synchronizing lab tests and reducing the batching of microbiological tests can help minimize many patients waiting time in a way that will accelerate emergency room overall flow and the capacity to take care of patients.

When flow increases, capacity also increases. The converse is not necessarily true: an increase in resource utilization won't automatically translate to an increase in flow. In the hospital example, the lab may do more tests per day in large batches but that won't necessarily mean that patients will get treated faster.

Local cost consideration is one of the major reasons for bad flow. In some environments it is more evident if we look at the policies that aim to achieve high local utilization of resources. We all assume that a resource standing idle is a waste. This perception results in efforts to maximize the output of every resource by artificially forcing a high level of resource utilization, typically in the form of producing for future demand. This mode of operation focuses on local efficiencies and not on the flow. Its immediate result is overproduction and an increase in work in process and queues that compromise the flow.

The first step in improving the flow is to take the right actions to prevent overproduction and local efficiencies. Once we cease making these mistakes, the next step is to focus on the major disturbances in flow and remove them. This will increase the system productivity as well as its flow. In order to increase flow, three major concepts need to be implemented:

> A practical mechanism to indicate when not to produce must be established

> Local efficiencies must be abolished

A focusing process to balance and improve
the flow should be put in place

To enhance the flow the first step is to establish
a mechanism to tell the operation when not to
produce. Preventing overproduction is necessary for reducing lead time, inventory and cost.
When Henry Ford invented the flow line he enhanced flow by limiting the actual space between
the different workstations. Ford's dedicated lines
are justified when the production volume is high
enough to support it. When the demand is more
fragmented, however, a different mechanism is
needed. Taiichi Ohno, the father of Toyota Production System, had a different mechanism. He used a
card-based replenishment system known as Kanban ("card" in Japanese). Every container has a
card that specifies its content. When a container
is withdrawn by the next workstation, its card is
passed back to the previous workstation and only
then production operation can start according to
the card's details. In essence, the Kanban system
directs each work center when and what to produce; more importantly, however, it directs when
not to produce. No card = no production. To make
the card system work and produce according to

the actual demand, reduction in setup times is necessary. The continuous effort to reduce setup time enhances the flow and productivity.

Ohno also introduced a process to improve the flow continuously. The fewer inventories on the shop floor, the more noticeable the presence of every disturbance, as each disturbance is likely to starve the next workstation. By gradually reducing the number of containers and parts per containers between two workstations, Ohno exposed the major disruption to flow and focused the improvement effort accordingly.

To implement the Kanban system successfully, the production and business environments should have a certain level of stability. Kanban systems are designed to run on very low "Just In Time" inventory. This requires the production floor to have a minimal amount of disturbances, since each local disturbance has the potential to starve the following workstation. The replenishment nature of the system also assumes that the product mix is stable. This is a reasonable assumption for a car manufacturer where the product life is long and the demand is relatively steady over time. However, it is not the case in many other businesses, such as consumer electronics, fashion, engineering tools or generic pharmaceutical. The last element of stability that the Kanban system requires is stability of orders over time. The Kanban system doesn't allow producing ahead of time, so if we have peaks and valleys in demand the production floor can oscillate between underutilization and overutilization based on the actuals orders flow. Again, it is less of an issue for a car manufacturer that sees relatively stable demand from its distribution network, but it can present real challenges in any other industry in which the orders are less scheduled.

Ford and Ohno developed different applications to prevent overproduction and enhance the flow. They demonstrated that by focusing on flow and reducing lead time an operation can run much more effectively. Their applications are suitable for stable environments, but what mechanism prevents overproduction and improves the flow in relatively unstable environments?

As Goldratt showed, the most intuitive basis for the mechanism to restrict overproduction is not space or inventory but time: if one wants to prevent production ahead of time, one should not release the material ahead of time.

The robustness of the time-based mechanism stems from the fact that it directly restricts the overall amount of work in the system rather than restricting the amount of work between any two workstations. Restricting the amount of work between two workstations increases the dependencies on the shop floor and thus makes it more susceptible to noise/disturbances. The time-based system also provides the flexibility required by many industries, since the production floor is not committed to replenishing the past demand.

The use of a time-based system requires that for each order we should restrict the release of the corresponding material to an appropriate amount of time before the due date of the order. But how does one go about computing the appropriate time?

The logical step is to look at the current production lead time. The problem is that the lead time is determined by the time of the release. The production lead time consists of the actual process time and the waiting time in queues in the different workstations. In a typical production environment, most of the lead time is waiting time. The earlier we release orders the more inventories we have in the system and the longer the lead time will be. If we expect our lead time to be long, and release orders too early, we will find that we are right. It is a typical case of a self-fulfilling prophecy.

To prevent overproduction, time-based mechanisms demand a counterintuitive action. We need to choke the release of materials and release them later than we used to, with a shorter time buffer than our current lead time. A good time buffer will be one that commands a ratio of 5 to 1 between the expected lead time and touch time. If we strive initially for a shorter lead time we may risk going to the other extreme and starve the floor. We are also likely to have a hard time meeting our promised due dates. Since the common lead time in many cases mandates a ratio of 10 to 1 between the lead time and the touch time, this means that in many cases to prevent overproduction we need to cut the lead time by half. This is very counterintuitive especially in environments that suffer from poor due date performance to start with.

The following example demonstrates the impact of cutting the release time by half. The graph was taken from a 2000-employee Chinese manufacturer of kitchenware. This company is a supplier of thousands of different products to major US retailers.

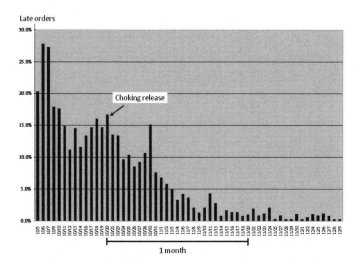

Cutting the release time by half is just the starting point. As we keep improving the flow by actions such as shrinking long setup operations, opening bottlenecks and improving the stability of unstable processes, we can and should cut the release buffer time and consequently the lead time further. We can use the time buffer to signal when it is the right time to do so.

The time buffer is used as a mechanism to focus the balancing and improvement of the flow. This is done by dividing the time buffer into three zones. We assign each third a different color: the first third is green, the second is yellow and the third is red. Late orders are marked black. We expect work orders to be completed across the different zones. Some will be finished in the green, some in the red, and some even after that in the black. As we take actions to fundamentally improve the flow we will see that more and more orders are completed earlier, in the green and yellow zones. This will be a good indication that we can cut the release time further. The color system also provides us a straightforward priority system. In the different queues, orders that are in the red should get a priority over orders that are in the yellow or the green. Monitoring the color status and following its priorities helps us improve due date performance and to identify disturbances to flow.

Ford with space, Ohno with inventory, and Goldratt with time: here are three different applications of the concept of preventing overproduction. Which application to use depends upon the assumptions about the operation and the business environment in which the company operates.

The concept of preventing overproduction is valid not only for production environments where the process time is small, but also to environments with high touch time, such as workshops and projects. These environments require a different application.

13
Bad multitasking

"Bad multitasking is the main blockage to flow in high touch time environments."

We admire the ability to multitask. Having the ability to deal with multiple challenges in parallel is a necessity for every manager. But excessive multitasking as a mode of operation has significant negative effects on the operation of the business.

Bad multitasking occurs when too many projects and/or too many tasks are open simultaneously. We know that we have too many when the common practice for the individuals is to jump back and forth between different tasks. We are in a state of bad multitasking when people too often stop working on a task before its natural completion point in order to promote another task that requires attention.

Bad multitasking prolongs the completion time of each task by three-to fourfold. This results in a large number of open activities that complicate the synchronization effort and break the flow. It also significantly compromises quality and the system's overall capacity.

To demonstrate the impact of bad multitasking let's look at an industry that many of us know as customers: the collision repair business. It is common to see a technician working on multiple vehicles in parallel. Typically for the following reasons: one vehicle is waiting for supplemental approval from the insurance company due to additional hidden damage that was found in the repair process, a second vehicle is waiting for a missing part, and the third vehicle is actually undergoing repair. As parts and approvals arrive the technician will juggle between the vehicles. This mode of operation helps to keep the technician busy but it creates havoc in the workshop.

Having multiple vehicles per technician jams the workshop floor. Parts are easily mixed and lost. Many times the quality of the work is also compromised. Moreover, in this mode of operation the technician is likely to finish the three vehicles in time proximity. In a short period of time all the three vehicles will wait in queue for paint. This means an artificial load in painting that usually will translate into a demand for more capacity in the paint booth. But this is not a capacity problem, it is a flow problem. The flow is very slow because of the disturbances that caused the technician to stop, such as missing approvals, and missing parts. The flow gets even slower as the technician moves back and forth between his vehicles. And as a result we get artificial peaks and queues that slow the flow even further.

To rectify the situation we need to remove the obstacles to flow. The first step is to ensure that every vehicle that is released to the shop floor can flow without a need to stop ("full kit" policy). i.e. all the necessary approvals and all the parts are available before the technician starts to work on the vehicle. This policy requires a more thorough inspection process, but here slow is fast. The second step is to create a queue mechanism where vehicles are released based on a given priority one at a time per technician, so that every technician can work on a given vehicle without any interruption. This will ensure that vehicles will flow continuously to the paint area without artificial peaks and minimum waiting time.

Another common example of bad multitasking can be shown in the operation of the court system. In cases where there is no jury, most of trial duration is waiting time between hearings. The more cases that are brought in front of the judges simultaneously the longer it will take between one hearing and another. This is not just because of the judge's need to jump between many cases but also because of the need to schedule the lawyers who are also engaged in many cases. The combination of multitasking as a mode of operation and dependencies between the different parties severely compromises the flow and prolongs the trial duration time.

When we jump back and forth between different tasks we do have a mental setup. The more intellect the task requires, the more likely we are to make mistakes. The likelihood of making mistakes is not limited to professions such as programmers, engineers, researchers and lawyers. There are numerous group exercises that demonstrate that multitasking even has a negative impact on the quality of simple physical tasks.

Partial staffing (allocating a partial team for a task) is also a form of bad multitasking. It is less obvious since resources are not being juggled between jobs as much, but this strategy still has a negative impact on the system flow.

Despite its massive negative impact, bad multi-tasking is the common mode of operation. This is due to cultural and behavioral norms. Most of the organizations whose main operation is projects have a matrix structure in which different resource groups serve different business units. It is the most efficient way of running an operation, and yet it tends to create conflicts over priorities. To get a better place in the lines the project managers tend to start their projects and its tasks as early as possible. This creates a glut of open tasks in the operation which results in bad multitasking. The ongoing daily fight over priorities just intensifies the problem by causing the resources to jump even more between tasks. The effort to appease everyone results in a lose-lose situation.

The pressure to open more tasks is not limited to the project managers. It also comes from the resources and their managers. When a resource is working on a task that gets stuck due to a missing part, approval, or definition, its immediate tendency is not to stand idle, but to pull another task to work on. When we let this behavior go on we end up with many tasks waiting in front of the resources. Some of these tasks are stuck in different stages waiting for missing elements. Some of them are fighting for the resource's attention.

We can't expect resources to embrace waiting idly for missing elements, but we can expect that projects and major tasks will be released with the adequate level of preparation that will enable them to flow. In other words, we can give them a full kit. It is the pressure to start projects as early as possible that causes us to release projects without a full kit. As these projects get stuck, we release even more projects. This intensifies the bad multitasking even further.

To reduce the level of bad multitasking and improve the flow we have to control the number of projects and tasks in the system. We have to implement mechanisms to guard against our natural inclination to release projects and tasks as early as possible. There are four mechanisms that need to be put in place:

Full kit; projects and major tasks like integration can be started only when their full kit is ready

Freeze in the project level; since the current reality is that there are too many projects in the system, we need to discover what the reasonable number is and freeze the rest based on business priorities.

Freeze in the projects' leg level; starting all projects' legs as early as possible also leads to artificial load in each project and on different resources. We have to release the leg based on a reasonable buffer so each leg will not delay integration with the critical chain and unnecessarily prolong the project's completion.

Freeze in the tasks' level: limit the number of open tasks a resource can have on its desk. This mechanism can also be applied in areas that are not typical project environments, such as lawyers' offices, loan officers, insurance claim processing centers, and even sales environments.

14
Measurements

"Tell me how you measure me and I will tell you how I behave."

Measurements drive behavior. This causes management to rely too often on measurements to manage.

Almost every single measurement on its own has the potential to cause a distortion in behavior leading to local/suboptimal results. Here are a few examples:

Earnings per share can lead to stock buyback and increased leverage level exactly when the company's total earning is down.

A conversion rate is an important measure for salespeople. But putting too much emphasis on it can push salespeople to pre-qualify the leads and even eliminate some.

Average margin per transaction is an important measure in the auto dealership industry, but forcing it on every transaction can cause the dealership to reject deals that can help boost the overall business.

Debt rating caused the financial industry to artificially create the desired rating, which helped to fuel the last debt crisis.

All the above measurements are not inherently wrong, but when we put too much emphasis on them, they push people to adopt distorted methods in order to meet these measurements, resulting in missing the desired objective for which the measurements were originally introduced.

One way to deal with the potential of distortion is to define the measurement as a part of a set of measurements that balance each other out, so that any distorted behavior that improves one measurement will have negative impact on the other measurement in the set. This approach can be applied in the case of earnings per share. In isolation, the measurement can be misleading, but with the right array of measurements, earnings per share can provide a good description of the actual picture.

Another approach to dealing with the potential of distortion is to use the measurements for control, but not for driving results. In this approach, management drives results by forcing employees to follow the required processes, and then using the measurements to make sure business is not going off course. This approach can be applied in cases such as conversion ratio and average margin per transaction. The conversion ratio and the transaction margins are the results of the right sales process. The focus should be on ensuring the sales process is followed. This is done by measuring the inputs of the sales force, which ensures that the sales force does not skip crucial steps in the process. Monitoring the output measurements is crucial to making sure that the flexibility the process provides is not taking the company off course.

A measurement like debt rating represents another challenge. Debt rating is part of a family of score measurements that are composed using different parameters. The problem with such score measurements is that they are not intuitive with respect to cause and effect. When the score changes we can't instantly say why. Moreover, oftentimes some of the parameters that constitute the score may change without affecting the overall score. These measurements are therefore susceptible to manipulation. A key number of parameters that should be monitored across a pre-defined scale with a color system indicator of red, yellow and green, should be substituted for score measurement, like debt rating.

We must eliminate the last group of measurements because they are just plain wrong. Following them will lead to the opposite of the desired result. Below are kinds of measurements that promote local optimum behavior:

Ton per hour, which is a common measurement in chemical and metal industries, can distort the production mix toward products that have high rate of ton per hour. Similar measurements are tire per hour, and tablets per month.

Cost per unit and productivity measurements also lead to local suboptimal results. They induce local efficiency behavior on the production shop floor resulting in inflated inventory and long lead time.

Number of fillings in the generic pharmaceutical industry ignores the potential value of each drug. This has the potential to skew the development efforts.

Measurements of local optimum behavior should be abolished and replaced with holistic measurements. For example, instead of ton per hour or any other production record measure, we should look at the ability of the company to supply on time. If the company produces to order we should look at on-time delivery as a measure. If the company produces to stock we should look at the stock buffer level as a measurement.

15
Resistance to change

"Overcoming resistance to change is a major challenge for any implementation. Yet dealing with it on a personal level is a mistake."

There is a known bias in social psychology, according to which people tend to overestimate personal factors and underestimate situational ones when explaining a certain behavior. This bias is especially counterproductive when it comes to dealing with resistance to change. When we face resistance to change we tend to blame the person resisting and not the nature of the change or the way it was presented.

This doesn't mean that personality has nothing to do with resistance to change. Change holds uncertainty and people differ in their levels of tolerance to uncertainty. Yet our aim is not to change peoples' personalities but to implement our suggested change.

The productive approach is to address the change as an offer we have to sell. We have to come up with an attractive offer so that the reasonable customer of the change will buy into it.

There are four aspects regarding the change that we have to consider when we build our offer. What are the pros and cons of the suggested change? What are the pros and cons of staying in the current situation? We have to answer these questions not from our perspective, but from the perspective of the individual/organization we are trying to convince.

What are the pros of change? What is the "pot of gold" in our offer? The answer can't be a laundry list of many small benefits. It should be something substantial and meaningful to the customer of the change.

What are the cons of the change? What are the risks that the change presents? Is the effort it requires in proportion to the ultimate benefit? Our offer should present a reasonable and containable level of risk and effort.

What are the pros of not changing? What are the good things in the current situation that we may have to ask the other parties to give up? The less we ask them to give up, the better our offer is. This point is often overlooked, especially when it comes to new technological products. We tend to focus on the pros of the new technology while ignoring or underestimating the benefits of the old one, such as its ease of use, mature infrastructure, number of components suppliers, compatibility with other systems and requirements.

What are the cons of not changing? What are the alligators in the current environment that will come and bite us if we don't change? The bigger the alligators, the bigger the risk of staying in the current situation. Even people who prefer the status quo will be more open to a change when the alligators are present. The challenge is that due to inertia, we tend to assume that the near future will look very much like the past. This often leads us to ignore or underestimate the presence of the alligators.

Taking all these aspects of the change into account to increase our ability to sell the change, we need to understand which of these four aspects of the change is blocking the customer from accepting our change and construct an offer that will emphasize how this concern is addressed.

When we think about big change, quitting smoking is definitely one of them. Here also is our tendency to personalize the change: "If you are strong enough you can quit, if you continue smoking you are weak." Allen Carr knew better. He was an accountant and a heavy smoker who found an easy way to stop smoking. It worked for him and for the millions who followed his approach and read his book. Carr's main insight was that the conventional approach highlights the reasons not to smoke, by emphasizing the negative consequences of smoking. This may be helpful in convincing people not to start smoking but it does not address the reasons why smokers do smoke, i.e. the good things that smokers receive from smoking. In our terminology, Carr understood that it is easier to convince smokers to stop smoking if we can show them that they do not lose the benefits they have in their current situation (the third aspect of the change). In his book, Carr covers all the perceived benefits smokers tend to have from smoking. One by one he demonstrates how these benefits can be obtained without smoking. This reduces the desire to smoke and the required willpower needed to quit smoking.

Designing an attractive offer is only the first part. We still need to sell it, which is another challenge. Even attractive offers do not sell themselves. Typically, a suggested change triggers multiple concerns in different stakeholders. Trying to discuss all these concerns concurrently is an impossible task, and often results in bigger confusion. To overcome this challenge, Goldratt suggested a Socratic-based buy-in process. The process contains six steps. Only when an agreement is achieved in one step can the discussion move to the next. The process aims to deal with resistance to change pillar by pillar. The steps in the process are the following:

Agreement on the problem. The definition of the problem is the gap between the current and the desired reality. The desired reality can be one in which the pot of gold is achieved or one in which the potential dangers, the alligators, are eliminated. The consensus we need to reach is why the gap exists. What is the conflict that prevents us from closing the gap?

Agreement on the direction of the solution. There

is more than one way to solve a conflict. Different assumptions can be challenged, which can lead to different solutions and approaches. To get a consensus on the right direction, we need to reach an agreement first on the criteria for a good solution. Once we have established the criteria, we create the reference to evaluate the direction of the solution and we are better positioned to reach an agreement on it.

Agreement on the solution. In this step we need to demonstrate that implementing the suggested solution will close the gap between the current and the desired states. The more stakeholders we have, the more emphasis we will have to put on the entirety of the solution, describing the meaning of closing the gap from the perspective of each stakeholder.

Yes, but. Dealing with the negative ramifications of the solution. The solution may be welcome but the side effects may be worse than the original problem. To get the required buy-in, we need to address the major "yes, but" reservations. Not all of them need to be solved completely but we do need to show that the risk or effort associated with them is manageable. Sometimes pilots or phased implementation helps to deal with such cases. Usually at this stage of the discussion people tend to mix their negative ramification reservations and the actual obstacles. It is important to separate between the two.

Obstacles. At this stage the main concern is how tangible the solution is. Typically, the discussion is about the different parts of the infrastructure that are missing. Our tendency is to argue about and negotiate the magnitude and importance of each obstacle. The right way to address this stage is to list all the obstacles and define for each one the intermediate objective that will overcome the obstacle. It is the discussion of the intermediate objectives that helps us ignore the negligible obstacles and focus the discussion on the important intermediate objectives and how to reach them.

Call to action. Once we translate each intermediate objective into an action plan, we need to synchronize and schedule the different action plans as part of one road map. This road map is necessary in order to make the call for action. But usually it is not enough. We still need to create the emotional commitment among the team members to start the implementation.